Paul Simon
Anthology

Amsco Publications
New York/London/Sydney

Cover Design by Pearce Marchbank Studios

Order No. PS 11196
US International Standard Book Number: 0.8256.1278.0
UK International Standard Book Number: 0.7119.2218.7

Exclusive Distributors:
Music Sales Corporation
257 Park Avenue South, New York, NY 10010 USA
Music Sales Limited
8/9 Frith Street, London W1V 5TZ England
Music Sales Pty. Limited
120 Rothschild Street, Rosebery, Sydney, NSW 2018, Australia

Printed in the United States of America by
Vicks Lithograph and Printing Corporation

Ace In The Hole

Words and Music by PAUL SIMON

Bm
A7
But I nev - er met the man, so I don't real - ly
down, dirt - y and des - p'rate, that's my e - mer - gen - cy bank -
knew that I was cra - zy. So I nev - er lost my self - con -
or - di - nar - y rhy - thm and blues, your ba - sic rock 'n'
Bm
A7
Bm
A7
know. May - be some Christ - mas, if I'm
roll. I got two hun - dred dol - lars, that's the
trol. I just walk in the mid - dle of the road; I
roll. You can sit on top of the beat; you can lean
Bm
A7
sick and a - lone, he will look up my
price on the street. If you wan - na get some
sleep in the mid - dle of the bed. I stop in the mid - dle
on the side of the beat; you can hang from the bot - tom

Bm
A7
num - ber, call me on the phone, and say,
qual - i - ty, that's the price you got to meet. And the man says,
of a sen-tence, and the voice in the mid-dle of my head said,
of the beat. But you got to ad-mit that the mu - sic is sweet.
G/D
Bm
F♯m
"Hey, boy.
"Hey, jun - ior.
"Hey, jun - ior.
Instrumental
Where you been so long?
G♯m7-5
Dm6/F
3fr.
Don't you know me? I'm your
1. 2.
A7
Bm
A7
Bm
A7
ace in the hole."

Bm
A7
Bm
A7
3.
ace in the hole,
A/E
D♯m7-5
Dmaj7
oh, yeah."
Ace in the
C♯m7-5
A♯°7
Bm7
To Coda
hole, lean on me. Don't you know me?
Dm6/F
3fr.
A
Bm7/A
I'm your guar - an - tee.

A7
Shuffle beat
G/D
G
F♯m
Rid-ing on this roll - ing bus,
be-neath a ston - y sky,
Bm
E7
A
with a slow moon ris - ing
and the smoke-stacks drift-ing by;
A7
G/D
G
in the hour when the heart is weak - est, and

F♯m
Bm
E7
mem-o-ry is strong;_ when time has stopped and the bus just_ rolls a-
A7
D
long. Roll on,_ roll on._
1.2.
A
3.
A
A/G♯
F♯m
Roll on,_ roll on._
Tempo I
Bm
E
Tacet
A7
Bm
A7
Bm
A7

Bm
A7
D.S. 𝄋 (no repeats) al Coda
Coda
Dm6/F
3fr.
I'm your guar - an - tee.
A

At The Zoo

Words and Music by Paul Simon

Gm
Bb
F7
Bb
D7
Gm
D7
(Hum)
(Hum)
Gm
Dm7
Bb
Gm
Dm7
Bb
Dm7
It's a light and tum-ble jour - ney, from the East - side to the park.
mf
Gm
Dm7
Bb
Dm
Gm
Dm7
F
F7
Just a fine and fan-cy ram-ble to the zoo.
Bb
D7
Gm7
Dm7
Bb
D7
Gm
Dm7
But you can take the cross - town bus, if it's rain - in' or it's cold, And the

B♭
D7
Gm
Dm7
C6
an - i - mals will love it, if you do, if you
Gm
C6
Gm
do. Oo Oo
Cmaj7
C7
Some-thing tells me, it's all hap - pen - ing At The Zoo.
mp
F
F7
B♭
F
Gm
I do be - lieve it, I do be - lieve it's true.

Dm7 Bb F7 Bb D7 Gm D7 Gm
(Hum) (Hum) Oh
Bb F7 Bb D7 Gm D7 Gm F7 Bb D7
(Hum) The mon-keys stand for
mf
Gm Dm7 Bb D7 Gm11 Gm Dm7 Bb D7
hon-es-ty, Gir-affes are in-sin-cere, And the el-e-phants are
Gm Dm7 F F7 Bb D7 Gm Dm7
kind-ly, but they're dumb. O-rang-u-tans are skep-ti-cal of

B♭
D7
Gm
Dm7
chan - ges in their ca - ges, And the zoo - keep - er is ve - ry fond — of
rum. ——
Ze - bras are re - ac - tion - a - ries, An - te - lopes are
mis - sion - a - ries, Pig - eons plot in se - cre - cy, — And ham - sters turn on
fre - quent - ly — What a gas! — You got - ta come and see — At The Zoo. —— At The
Repeat and fade

America

Words and Music by PAUL SIMON

Gm7
C7
Gm7
bought a pack of cig - a - rettes,
And Mrs.
Wag - ner's
C9
Gm7
F
Eb
Bb
pies,
And walked
off
to look for A -
Eb
Ebmaj7
Cm
Cm7
Ab
mer - i - ca.
Eb
Ebmaj7
"Kath - y," I said, As we

Cm
Eb
Ab
board - ed a Grey - hound in Pitts - burgh,
Eb
Ebmaj7
"Mich - i - gan seems like a dream to me now.
Cm7
Bb
It took me four days To hitch - hike from
F
Bb
F
Ebmaj7
Sag - i - naw. I've come to look for A - mer -

E♭
D♭maj7
i - ca." Laugh - ing on the
D♭
E♭
bus, Play-ing games with the fac - es,
D♭maj7
She said the man in the gab - ar-dine
E♭
suit Was a spy.

Ab
Abmaj7
Eb
I said, "Be care - ful, His bow - tie is real - ly a cam - 'ra."
Ebmaj7
Cm7
Eb6
Cm6(sus)
E
Abmaj7
Eb
Ebmaj7
Cm
"Toss me a cig - a - rette, I think there's
Eb
Ab
one in my rain - coat."

Eb
Ebmaj7
Cm
"We smoked the last one An hour a - go."
Gm7
Gm7
C9
So I looked at the scen - er - y,
She read her mag - a - zine;
And the
F
Eb
Bb
Eb
Ebmaj7
moon rose o - ver an o - pen

Cm7
Eb
Ab
field.
Eb
Ebmaj7
Cm
Eb
"Kath - y, I'm lost I said, Though I knew she was
Ab
Abmaj7
Fm7
Ab
Eb
sleep - ing. I'm emp - ty and
Ebmaj7
Cm
ach - ing and I don't know why."

B♭
F
Count - ing the cars On the New Jer - sey Turn - pike. They've all
B♭
F
E♭maj7
come to look for A - mer - i -
E♭
F
B♭
ca, All come to
Repeat and fade.
F
E♭maj7
E♭
look for A - mer - i - ca.

April Come She Will

Words and Music by PAUL SIMON

Am
Em
G
C
G
arms a-gain.
to her flight.
G
C
G
C
G
C
G
Am
Em
Au - gust, die she must, The au-tumn winds blow chil-
Fmaj7
Em
C
D
G
Em
- ly and cold; Sep-tem - ber I'll re - mem - ber.
Am
Em
D
G
A love once new has now grown old.
p

The Boxer

Words And Music by PAUL SIMON

Am
G
F
All lies and jest, still a man hears what he wants to hear, And
C
G
dis - re - gards the rest.
C
When I left my home and my fam - i - ly, I was

Am
G
no more than a boy in the com - pa - ny of stran - gers in the
Dm7
C
qui - et of a rail - way sta - tion run - ning scared,
Am
C
F
Lay - ing low, seek - ing out the poor - er quar - ters where the
G
F
Em
Dm
rag - ged peo - ple go, Look-ing for the plac - es on - ly they would

C
Am
know.
Lie - la - lie,
Lie - la -
G
Am
G
lie la lie - la - lie lie - la - lie
Lie - la -
F
G
C
lie la la la la Lie - la la la la lie.
Ask - ing on - ly work - man's wag - es I come

Am
G
look-ing for a job, but I get no of - fers,
Just a
Dm7
C
come-on from the whores on Sev-enth Av - e - nue.
Am
Dm7
G
F
I do de - clare, there were times when I was so lone-some I
C
G
took some com-fort there. Ooo - la - la la - la la la.

C
C
Then I'm lay - ing out my
G7
C
Am
G
win - ter clothes and wish - ing I was gone, go - ing home
Dm7
G7
G
C
Where the New York Cit - y win - ters are - n't bleed - ing me,
Em
Am
Lead - ing me,

G
C
go - ing home.
C
In the clear - ing stands a box - er, and a fight - er by his
Am
G
G7
trade, And he car - ries the re - mind - ers of ev - 'ry glove that
C
Dm7
G7
C
laid him down Or cut him till he cried out in his an - ger and his shame,

Am
G
F
C
"I am leav - ing, I am leav - ing." But the fight - er still re-mains.
G
C
G
F
C
Lie - la
Fade
Am
G
Am
lie, Lie - la - lie la lie - la - lie Lie - la - lie
G
F
C
Lie - la lie la la la la lie - la la la la lie. Lie - la

Wednesday Morning, 3 A.M.

Words and Music by PAUL SIMON

C
F
sleep with the night, And her hair, in a
rise, gent - ly fall, For I know with the
Dm
Bb
Am
fine mist floats on my pil - low, Re -
first light of dawn I'll be leav - ing, And to -
F
Gm
Bb
C
flect - ing the glow of the win - ter moon -
night will be all I have left to re -
F
Gm
light.
call.

F
1.
2.
2. She is
3. Oh,
(4. My)
F Dm B♭ Am
what have I done,___ Why have I done it,___
life seems un - real,___ my crime an il - lu - sion,___
F Gm C
I've com - mit - ted a crime,___ I've brok - en the law,
A scene bad - ly writ - ten in which I must play,
F Dm B♭ Am
For___ twen - ty - five dol - lars and piec - es of sil - ver,___
Yet I___ know as I gaze at my young love be - side me,___

F
1. Gm
Bb
C
I held up and robbed a hard liq - uor
The morn - ing is
F
Gm
F
store.
4. My
2. Gm
Bb
C
just a few hou - - rs a -
F
Gm
F
way.
rit.
p

Bridge Over Troubled Water

Words and Music by PAUL SIMON

Eb
Ab
Bb
Cm
I'm on your side. Oh,
I'll take your part. Oh,
mp
Bb9
Eb (D bass)
In tempo
Eb7
Eb9
F
when times get rough
when dark-ness comes
And friends just can't be found,
And pain is all a-round,
f
Eb7
F#dim (A bass)
Eb (Bb bass)
C7sus
C7
Like a Bridge O-ver Trou-bled Wa-ter
G7
I will lay me down. Like a Bridge O-ver Trou-bled Wa-ter
mf

Ab
Bb9 (sus)
Bb7
Eb
Ab
I will lay me down.
mf
f
Eb
Ab
Eb
Ab
Rubato
When you're
mf
mp
mf
mp
p
2
Eb (Bb bass)
Cm
Ab
Cm (G bass)
G
Cm
F7
Trou-bled Wa-ter I will lay me down.
mf
f
Eb
Ab
Cm
Ab
Abm
Eb

Ab
Eb
Ab
Eb
Ab
Sail on
Eb
sil - ver girl,
Sail on by.
Ab
Db
Ab
Your time has
Eb
Ab
Eb
Ab
Eb
Ab
come to shine.
All your dreams are on their way.
Eb
Bb
Cm
Bb
Eb
Eb
(D bass)
See how they shine.
Oh,
if you need a friend
mp

In tempo

Eb7 Eb9 Ab F Bb Eb7 Eb9 Ab F#dim (A bass)

I'm sail - ing right be - hind. Like a Bridge O - ver

f

Eb (Bb bass) Cm Ab Cm G Cm Eb7 Eb9 Ab Abmaj7 F7 (A bass)

Trou-bled Wa-ter I will ease your mind. Like a Bridge O - ver

mf f ff

Eb (Bb bass) Cm Ab G7 Cm F9 Fmaj9

Trou - bled Wa-ter I will ease your mind.

Eb (Bb bass) Ab Abm Eb

rall.

fff

Congratulations

Words and Music by PAUL SIMON

E+
F
A
D
I don't know when,
oh, and I don't know
G
C
D
G
when,
oh, and I don't know when.
C
D
G
D
I no-tice so man-y peo-ple
D7
Em
C#7-5
C6
slip-pin' a-way,
And
3

Bm
Am
G
G (F bass)
C (E bass)
many more waiting in the lines
in the
E+
F
A
D
court - rooms to - day,
oh, in the
G
C
G
court - rooms to - - day.
G7
A
D
Love is not a game, love is not a toy, love's no ro -

G
C
G7
- mance.
A
D
G
Love will do you in, and love will wash you out, and need - less to say you
D
(F# bass)
Em
A7
D
won't stand a chance,
and you won't stand a chance.
Em
Fm
A11
D
I'm hun - gry for learn - - in',

D
(C# bass)
D7
Em
C#m7-5
Won't you ans - wer me, please.
C6
Bm
Am
G
G
(F bass)
C
(E bass)
Can a man and a wo - man live to -
E+
F
A
D
geth - er in peace,
oh, live to-geth-er in peace?
G
C
D
G
ritard.

Cecilia

Words and Music by PAUL SIMON

B♭
F
1. C
2. C
beg-ging you please_ to come home._
_ Ho - ho - home._
mp
F
B♭
_ Mak-ing love_ in the af - ter - noon_ with Ce-ci -
F
B♭
F
C
F
(mak - ing love___)
- lia, Up in my___ bed - room,_ I got up___ to wash_
B♭
F
C
F
___ my face_ When I come back to bed,_ some-one's tak - en my place._

F
B♭
Cel - ia, You're break-ing my heart, You're shak-ing my con - fi - dence dai -
mf
C
- ly. Oh, Ce - cil - ia, I'm down on my knees, I'm
beg-ging you please to come home. Come on home. Poh poh
mp
Fsus
poh poh poh poh poh poh poh poh poh poh poh. Ju - bi -

B♭
F
la - tion, She loves me a - gain,
I fall on the floor and I laugh-
f
mf
C
ing.
Ju - bi -
ing.
Oh oh
oh oh oh
oh oh oh oh
oh
oh oh oh oh
oh oh oh
oh.
Come on home.
rall.

Cloudy

Words and Music by PAUL SIMON

D
Dmaj7
Ddim
think it's hang - in' down on me. And it's a
bor - ders, no bound - a - ries. They
A7
F♯m
A
hitch-hike a hun - dred miles. I'm a rag - a - muf - fin
ech - o and they swell. From Tol - stoi to Tin - ker
Bm
E
E7
child. Point - ed fin - ger - paint - ed smile.
Bell. Down from Berke - ley to Car - mel.
A
A7
I left my shad - ow wait - in' down the
Got some pic - tures in my pock - et and a

1.
F♯m
A7
2.
F♯m
A7
D
road for me a while.
lot of time to kill, Hey sunshine
Dmaj7
Gsus4
G
I haven't seen you in a long time. Why don't you
D
Dmaj7
Ddim
show your face and bend my mind? These
A7
F♯m
A
clouds stick to the sky like a float - ing ques - tion,

Bm
E
E7
why?
And they lin - ger there to die.
A
A7
They don't know where they're go - ing, and, my
F♯m
A7
D
friend, nei - ther do I,
Cloud - y,
Repeat and fade out
G
Cloud - y.

Duncan

Words and Music by PAUL SIMON

D
Em
song, here's my song.
Em
D
2. My fath - er was a fish - er - man, my ma - ma was a fish - er - man's friend, And
G
A
D
I was born in the bore - dom and the chow - der, So
C
G
C
G
when I reached my prime, I left my home in the Mar - i - times,

C
G
D
Em
Head - ed down the turn - pike for New Eng - land,__ sweet New Eng - land.
C
G
C
G
C
Instrumental solo
G
Em
D
Em
Em
D
3 Holes in my con - fi - dence,_ holes in the knees of my jeans, I's

G A D C G

left with - out__ a pen - ny in my pock - et, Oo hoo hoo__ wee,_ I's a - bout

C G C G

des - ti - tut - ed as a kid could be,__ And I wished I wore a ring so I could

D Em

hock it,__ I'd like to hock it. 4. A

Em D

young girl in a park - ing lot__ was preach - in' to a crowd,_ sing - in'

G
A
D
sa - cred songs and read - ing from the Bi - ble,
Well, I
C
G
C
G
told her I was lost,
and she told me all a - bout the Pen - te - cost,
And I
C
G
D
seen that girl as the road to my sur - vi
Em
C
G
C
val.
Instrumental solo

G
C
G
Em
D
Em
Em
5. Just lat - er on the ver - y same night when I
D
G
A
crept to her tent with a flash - light, And my long years of in - no - cence
D
C
G
end - ed,
Well, she took me to the woods, say - in',

C
G
C
G
"Here comes some - thin' and it feels so good!" And just like a dog I was be -
D
Em
friend - ed, I was be - friend - ed.
Em
D
6. Oh, oh, what a night, oh, what a gar - den of de - light, Ev - en
G
A
D
now that sweet mem - o - ry ling - ers, I was

C
G
C
G
5
play - in' my gui - tar,___ ly - ing un - der - neath the stars,___ Just
5
C
G
D
Em
thank - in' the Lord for my fin - gers,___ for my fin - gers.
Fade out
C
G
C
G
C
G
Em
D
Em

Diamonds On The Soles Of Her Shoes

Words and Music by PAUL SIMON
Beginning by PAUL SIMON and JOSEPH SHABALALA

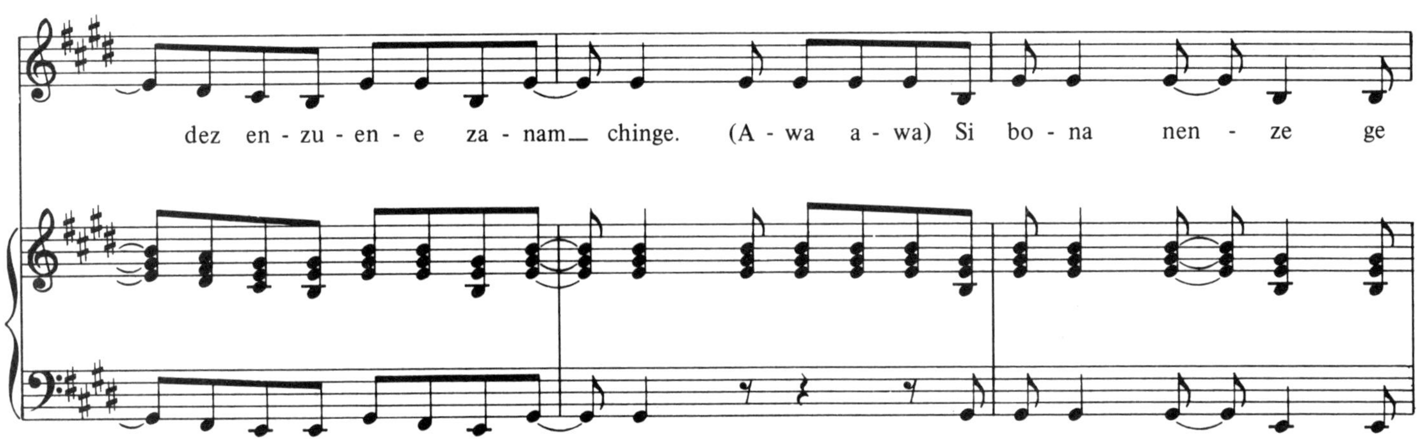

E
girl, she don't try to hide it; dia - monds on the soles of her shoes.
He's a poor boy, emp - ty as a pock-et, emp-
A
ty as a pock-et with noth - ing to lose. Sing ta na na, ta
E
B
E
na na na. She got dia - monds on the soles of her shoes. Ta

A
E
B
na na,
ta na na
na.
She got dia - monds on the soles of her shoes,
E
A
E
dia - monds on the soles of her shoes,
dia -
B
E
B
monds on the soles of her shoes,
dia - monds on the soles of her shoes,
E
A
E
dia - monds on the soles of her shoes.

Slightly faster
Tacet
F
B♭
C
People say she's crazy, she got
She makes the sign of the teaspoon,
diamonds on the soles of her shoes.
he makes the sign of the wave.
Well, that's one way to lose these
The poor boy changes clothes and he puts on
walking blues,
after shave
diamonds on the soles of her shoes.
to compensate for his ordinary shoes.

B♭ C F B♭ C
She was phys - i - c'lly_for - got - ten, and then she slipped in - to_ my pock - et with my car
And she said, "Hon - ey, take_me danc - ing, but they end - ed up_ by sleep - ing in a door -
F B♭ C F
keys._ She said, "You've tak - en me for grant - ed be - cause I please_ you, wear - ing these
way___ by the bo - de - gas and the lights on up - per Broad - way, wear - ing
B♭ C F B♭ C
dia - monds."
dia - monds on___ the___ soles of their___ shoes.___
And I could say
F B♭ C F
oo.
As if
And

B♭
C
F
ev - 'ry - bod - y knows what I'm talk - ing a - bout.
As if
I mean
B♭
C
F
3
ev - 'ry - bod - y here would know ex - act - ly what I was talk - ing a - bout.
Talk - in' 'bout
3
B♭
C
F
B♭
C
dia - monds on the soles of her shoes.
F
F/B♭
B♭/C
C
F
F/B♭
B♭/C
C

F
B♭
C
People say I'm crazy, I got diamonds on the soles of my shoes.
Well,
that's one way to lose these walking blues.
Diamonds on the soles of my shoes.
Repeat and fade
Ta na na na na,
ta na na na na.

The 59th Street Bridge Song
(Feelin' Groovy)

Words and Music by PAUL SIMON

E♭
B♭
Cm7sus
B♭
E♭
B♭
Cm7
B♭
look-in' for fun and Feel - in' Groov - y.
E♭
B♭
Cm7sus
B♭
E♭
B♭
Hel - lo lamp - post, what - cha know - in' I've come to watch your flow -
Cm7sus
B♭
E♭
B♭
Cm7sus
B♭
- ers grow - in'. Ain't - cha got no rhymes for me?
E♭
B♭
Cm7sus
B♭
E♭
B♭
Cm7sus
B♭
Doot - in' doo - doo, Feel - in' Groov - y. Got

Eb
Bb
Cm7sus
Cm7
no deeds to do, no prom - is - es to keep. I'm dap - pled and drow - sy and
read - y to sleep. Let the morn - ing - time drop all its pet - als on me.
Life, I love you, All is groov - y.
Repeat and fade out

Everything Put Together Falls Apart

Words and Music by PAUL SIMON

Dm7
Cmaj7
Em7
Am
Em
D (F♯ bass)
uh huh, I ain't blind, no, some folks are
Dm (F bass)
Dm7
G7
C7
cra - zy, oth - ers walk that bor - der line, watch what you're do - in', Tak - in'
Fm7
Cadd9
F7
Cm7 (F bass)
downs to get off to sleep, and ups to start you on your
B♭
B
B♭
A
E
way; Af - ter a while they'll change your style,

E7 A Am Em F♯m E A E7

Mm I see it hap-pen-in ev-'ry day.

Dm7 Cmaj7 Em7 Am E D (F ♯ bass)

Uh huh, spare your heart. ev-'ry-thing

Dm (F bass) Dm7 G7 C7

put to-geth-er soon-er or lat-er falls a-part, there's noth-in'

C F7 Cm7 (F bass)

lie, For all the good it-'ll do you, you can die,

B♭ B B♭ A

Oh, but when it's done and the po-lice come, and they're lay-

E E7 A Am

-in' you down for dead, Uh huh, just re-

Em F♯m E E7 A Am Em F♯m7 E

mem-ber what I said!

Flowers Never Bend With The Rainfall

Words and Music by PAUL SIMON

C
G
Bm7
Cmaj7
I don't know what is real, I can't touch what I
I am blind-ed by the light of God and truth and
So my fan-ta-sy be-comes re-al-i-
G
Bm
Cmaj7
G
C
G
feel And I hide be-hind the shield of my il-lu-sion.
right And I wan-der in the night with-out di-rec-tion.
ty, And I must be what I must be and face to-mor-row.
Chorus:
D
C
G
So I'll con-tin-ue to con-tin-ue
Em
C6
to pre-tend My life will nev-er

Em
A
C
end,
And Flow - ers
Nev - er Bend
G
1.2.
With The Rain - fall.
2. The
3. No
3.
rall.
p
C9add11

Gone At Last

Words and Music by PAUL SIMON

C
G7
C
G7
C
stopped to rest for a while. I sat down at a
grabbed my sym - pa - thy. Sweet lit - tle soul now what's your
bur - dens will be shared. Yes, I do be - lieve if I had - n't
C7
F
C
truck stop; I was think - in' a - bout my past.
prob - lem, tell me why you're so down - cast.
met you, I might still be sink - ing fast.
I've had a
C7
F
C
G7
long streak of bad luck, but I'm pray - in' it's gone at
C
C
last. Gond, gone at last, gone at last, gone at

F
C
last. gone at last. I've had a long streak of that
C7
F
To Coda
C
G7
1.
C
bad luck but I'm pray - in' it's gone at last. I ain't
2.
C
3.
C
D. S. al Coda
Coda
C
last. Ev - 'ry once in a last. Gone, gone at pray - in' it's
G7
C
gone at last.

For Emily, Whenever I May Find Her

Words and Music by PAUL SIMON

C
F
rain.
I wan - dered emp - ty streets down
Bb
F
passed the shop dis - plays.
I heard ca -
Eb
Bb
the - dral bells
trip - ping down the al - ley ways,
as I
C
F
walked on.
And when you ran to me your
mf

B♭
F
cheeks flushed with the night.
We walked on
E♭
frost - ed fields
of ju - ni - per and lamp - light,
B♭
C
I held your hand.
F
B♭
And when I a - woke and felt you warm and near,

F
Eb
I kissed your hon - ey hair with my grate-ful
Bb
C
tears. Oh I love you, girl.
Eb
Bb
Bbmaj9
Oh, I love
you.

Graceland

Words and Music by PAUL SIMON

E
B
A
E
land, Grace - land in Mem-phis, Ten-nes - see. I'm go - ing to Grace - land.
land, Mem-phis, Ten-nes - see. I'm go - ing to Grace - land.
land, Grace - land. I'm go - ing to Grace - land.
D
A
E
Poor boys and pil - grims with
Poor boys and pil - grims with
For rea - sons I can - not ex - plain, there's some
B
A
E
fam - i - lies and we are go - ing to Grace - land.
fam - i - lies and we are go - ing to Grace - land.
part of me wants to see Grace - land.

D A E
My trav - 'ling com - pan - ion is
My trav - 'ling com - pan - ions are
And I may be o - bliged to de - fend ev - 'ry
B A E
nine years old. He is the child of my first mar - riage.
ghosts and emp - ty sock - ets. I'm look - in' at ghosts and emp - ties.
love, ev - 'ry end - ing or may - be there's no ob - li - ga - tions, now.
D A E
But I've rea - son to be - lieve we both
But I've rea - son to be - lieve we all
May - be I've a rea - son to be - lieve we all

B
A
E
To Coda
D
A
will be re - ceived in Grace - land.
will be re - ceived in Grace - land.
will be re - ceived in Grace - land.
E
She comes back to tell me she's gone.
There is a girl in New York Cit - y who
A
As if I did - n't know that, as if I did - n't know my own
calls her - self the hu - man tram - po - line, and

C♯m
4fr.
B
bed,
as if I'd nev - er no - ticed
some-times when I'm fall - ing, fly - ing or tum - bl - ing in tur - moil I say, oh, so this is what she
E
0 00
the way she brushed her hair from her fore - head.
And she said
means. She means we're bounc - ing in - to Grace-land.
And I see
A
0 0
los - ing love is like a win - dow in your heart.
los - ing love is like a win - dow in your heart.

C♯m
4fr.
Ev - 'ry - bod - y sees you're blown a - part,
Ev - 'ry - bod - y sees you're blown a - part,
ev - 'ry - bod - y sees the
ev - 'ry - bod - y feels the
B
1.
A
2.
A
D.S. al Coda
wind blow.
wind blow.
I'm go - ing to Grace -
I'm go - ing to Grace -
Repeat and fade
Coda
D
A
E
B
A
E
D
A

Kathy's Song

Words and Music by PAUL SIMON

G
Bm
G
C
Soft and warm con - tin - u - ing
I gaze be - yond the rain - drenched streets
They lie with you when you're a - sleep
Am
Em
D
Tap - ping on my roof and
To Eng - land where my heart
And kiss you when you start your
G
C
G
G
C
G
walls.
lies.
day.
G
C
G
4. And a song I was writ - ing is left un - done
5. And so you see I have come to doubt
6. And as I watch the drops of rain

Am
Em
C
Bm7
I don't know why I spend my time
All that I once held as true
Weave their wear - y paths and die
G
Bm
G
C
writ - ing songs I can't be - lieve
I stand a - lone with - out be - liefs
I know that I am like the rain
Am
Em
D
G
C
With words that tear and strain. to rhyme.
The on - ly truth I know is you.
There but for the grace of you go I.
G
G
C
1.2.
G
3.
G
C
G

A Hazy Shade Of Winter

Words and Music by PAUL SIMON

C
Dm
C
hard to please, But look a-round, leaves are brown And the sky
Bb
A7
Dm
is A Ha - zy Shade Of Win - ter.
Hear the Sal-va-tion
C
Bb
Ar-my Band,
Down by the riv-er-side, It's bound to be a bet-ter ride, than
Am
C
what you've got planned, Car-ry your cup in your hand,
And look a-round,

Dm
C
Bb7
A7
leaves are brown now, And the sky is a Ha - zy Shade Of Win -
Dm
C
- ter. Hang on - to your hopes, my friend,
Bb
Am
That's an eas - y thing to say, but if your hopes should pass a - way, Simp - ly pre - tend that you can
3
C
Dm
C7
build them a - gain. Look a - round; The grass is high, the fields are

B♭7
A7
Dm
ripe: It's the spring - time of my life.
B♭
F
Fmaj7
Sea - sons change with the scen - er - y,
Weav - ing time in a
C9
Dm
A7
Dm
tap - es - try.
Won't you stop and re - mem - ber me,
C
B♭
At an - y con - ven - ient time?
Fun - ny how my mem - 'ry skips, while

Am
C
look-in' o-ver man-u-scripts of un-pub-lished rhyme,
Drink-ing my vod-ka and lime.
Dm
C7
Bb7
I look a-round
Leaves are brown now,
And the sky
is A Ha-
A7
Dm
C
Bb7
-zy Shade Of Win-ter.
Look a-round;
Leaves are brown,
There's a patch
1. A7
Dm
2. A7
Dm
of snow on the ground.
Look a-round;
of snow on the ground.

Hearts and Bones

Words and Music by PAUL SIMON

choose, are trav - 'lling to - geth - er in the
door, two peo - ple were mar - ried. The
coasts to re - sume old ac - quaint - anc - es,
San - gre de Chris - to, the Blood of Christ
act was out - ra - geous. The bride was con -
step out oc - ca - sion - al - ly and spec - u - late
B
Moun - tains of New Mex - i - co,
ta - gious. She burned like a bride.
who had been dam - aged the most.
Bm7
C♯m7
4 fr.
D♯m7-5
on the last leg of a jour - ney
These e - vents may have had some ef -
Eas - y time will de - ter - mine if

D♯°7
C♯m7
4fr.
they start - ed a long time a - go,
fect on the man with the girl by his side,
these con - so - la - tions will be their re - ward,
C♯m6
3fr.
Bmaj7
the arc of a love af - fair,
the arc of a love af - fair,
the arc of a love af - fair
Amaj9
rain - bows in the high des - ert
his hands roll - ing down her
wait - ing to be re -

air.
hair.
stored.
E
Moun - tain pass - es slip - ping in - to stones,
Love like light - ning shak - ing till it moans,
You take two bod - ies and you twirl them in - to one,
A
To Coda
hearts and bones,
E
G♯m7/D♯
4 fr.
hearts and

C♯m
4 fr.
bones,
hearts and
1.
E
bones.
Think - ing
2.
A(addB)
A
A(addB)
A
bones,
hearts and

E
bones.
And
E
F♯m
E/G♯
A
E
whoa_ whoa_ whoa,_ she_ said, "Why,
R.H.
why don't_ we drive through the night,_ and we'll

A
wake up down in Mex - i - co?
E
Oh I,
I don't know noth - in' a - bout, noth - in' a - bout no
A
Mex - i - co.
Tell me

E
why, why won't you love me for
A
who I am where I am?"
Am
He said, "'Cause that's not the way the world is, ba-
E/G♯
by. This is how I love

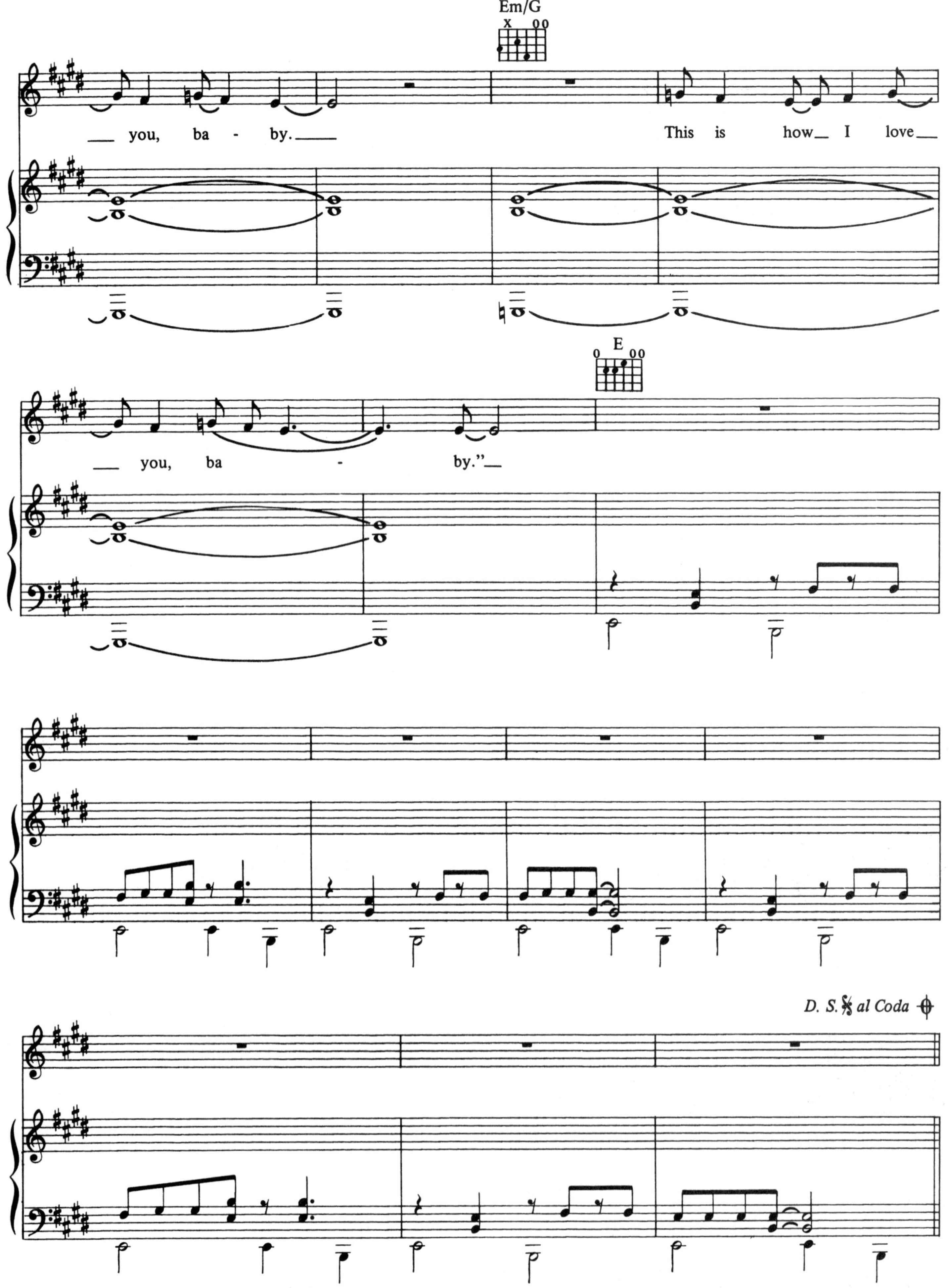

Em/G
x 00
you, ba - by.
This is how I love
you, ba - by."
E
0 00
D. S. al Coda

Coda
E
their hearts and their bones,
and they won't come un-
A
done,
hearts and bones,
E
G♯m7/D♯
4 fr.
hearts and bones,

C♯m
4 fr.
A(addB)
hearts and bones,
E
hearts and bones.

E
0
00
1.2.3.
4.

Hey, Schoolgirl

Words and Music by PAUL SIMON and ARTHUR GARFUNKEL

G
C
G
D7
to say, "Who-bop-a-loo-chi-bop, let's meet af-ter school at
G
1.2.
C
G
three."
1. She said, "Hey, babe, but there is one thing more,
2. She said, "Hey, babe, I got-ta lot to do,
D7
G
C
My school is o-ver at a half-past four,
It takes me ho-urs till my home-work's thru,
May-be when we're old-er, then
Some-day we'll go stead-y, so
G
D7
G
we can date,
don't you fret,
Ooh,
Ooh,
let's wait!"
not yet!"

3.
C
G
3. Then she turned a-round to me with that gleam in her eye,
D7
G
She said, "I'm sor-ry if I passed you by, I'm gon-na
C
G
D7
skip my home-work, gon-na cut my class,
Bug out of here
G
G
D7
G
E♭
C
real fast." Hey, School-girl in the sec-ond row,

G D7

Now we're go - in' stead - y, hear the words that I want_ you to

G Eb C C

know. Well, it's "Who - bop - a - loo - chi - bop,

G D7 G

you're mine, I knew it all the time."

Fade out

D7 G

Who - bop - a - loo - chi - bop, hah, you're mine.

How The Heart Approaches What It Yearns

Words and Music by PAUL SIMON

B7
E
how the heart ap-proach-es what it yearns.
In a
E
E9
fe - ver, I dis-tinct - ly hear your voice e-
Instrumental
phone booth in some lo - cal bar and grill, re-
A
E
merg - ing from a dream. The dream re - turns.
hears - ing what I'll say, my coin re - turns.
B7
To Coda
E
E7
How the heart ap-proach-es what it yearns.
I
How the heart ap-proach-es what it

G♭maj7
G♭/F
B♭m7
B♭m6
Cm7-5
C°7
Af - ter the rain on the In - ter-state, head - lights slide past the
dream we are ly - ing on the top of a hill and head - lights slide past the
B♭m7
E♭m7-5
D♭maj7
4fr.
moon. A bone - wea - ry trav - 'ler that waits by the side of the
moon. I roll in your arms and your voice is the heat of the
G♭maj7
G♭m6
1.
B7
2.
B7
D.S. al Coda
road: where's he go-ing? In a
night. I'm on fire.

Coda
E
B7
yearns.
How the heart ap-
proach - es
what it yearns.
E
B7
E
B7
E
rit.

I Am A Rock

Words and Music by PAUL SIMON

Dm7
Em7
Dm
F
G
F
To the streets be - low On a fresh - ly fall - en si - lent shroud of snow.
Friend-ship caus - es pain. It's laugh - ter and it's lov - ing I dis - dain.
feel - ings that have died. If I nev - er loved I nev - er would have cried.
Safe with - in my womb. I touch no one and no one touch - es me.
I Am A Rock,
f
C
F
G7
1.2.3.
C
I am an is - land.
Am
4.
C
2. I've built
3. Don't talk of
4. I have my land.
And a
mf
mf
Dm7
G7
C
Dm7
G7
C
rock feels no pain; And an is-land nev - er cries.
p

I Know What I Know

Words by PAUL SIMON
Music by PAUL SIMON and GENERAL M.D. SHIRINDA

G
C
F
right in a sort of a lim - it - ed way_ for an off night. She said,
kind of a girl who could say things that were - n't that fun - ny. I said,
"Are - n't you the wom - an who was re - cent - ly giv - en a Ful - bright?" She said,
G
C
F
"Don't I know_you from the cin - e - mat - o - graph - er's par - ty?" I said,
"What does that_ mean, I real - ly re - mind you of mon - ey?" She said,
"Don't I know you from the cin - e - mat - o - graph - er's par - ty?" I said,
G
C
F
"Who am I to blow a - gainst_ the wind?"_
"Who am I to blow a - gainst_ the wind?"_
"Who am I to blow a - gainst_ the wind?"_
I know what I_ know._

G
C
F
I'll sing what I said. We come and we go.
G
C
F
It's a thing that I keep in the back of my head. I know what I know.
G
C
F
I'll sing what I said. We come and we go.
G
C
F
G
It's a thing that I keep in the back of my head.

C
F
G
x000
To Coda
1.
She said, "There's
2.
D.S. al Coda
She
Coda
I know what I know.
Repeat and fade
I know what I know.
I know what I know.

KODACHROME™

WORDS AND MUSIC BY PAUL SIMON

• "KODACHROME" is a registered trademark for color film.

C7
F
Gm
C7
I can think at all.
And though my lack
F
Fmaj7
F7
F7+9
B♭
of ed - u - ca - tion has - n't hurt me none,
Gm
C7
I can read the writ - ing on the wall.

F
F7
Chorus:
B♭
D7
G7
Ko - da - chrome, They give us those nice
Cm
F
B♭
bright col - ors, They give us the greens of sum -
E♭
C
F
- mers, Makes you think all the world's a sun - ny
B♭
D
G
Cm
day. Oh yeah, I got a Ni - - kon

F
B♭
E♭
cam - 'ra, I love to take a pho - to - graph, So mom - ma, don't take
C7
F
B♭
my Ko - da - chrome a - way.
To next strain
Dm
Gm
C
No chord
2. If you took all
Fine
Verse 2.
F
Fmaj7
C7
F7+9
B♭
the girls I knew when I was sin - gle

Gm
C7
And brought them all to - geth - er for one
F
Gm
C7
F
Fmaj7
night,
I know they'd nev - er match my
F7
F7+9
B♭
sweet im - ag - i - na - tion,
Gm
C7
F
F7
D.S. al Fine
And ev - 'ry - thing looks worse in black and white. Ko - da -

JONAH

WORDS AND MUSIC BY PAUL SIMON

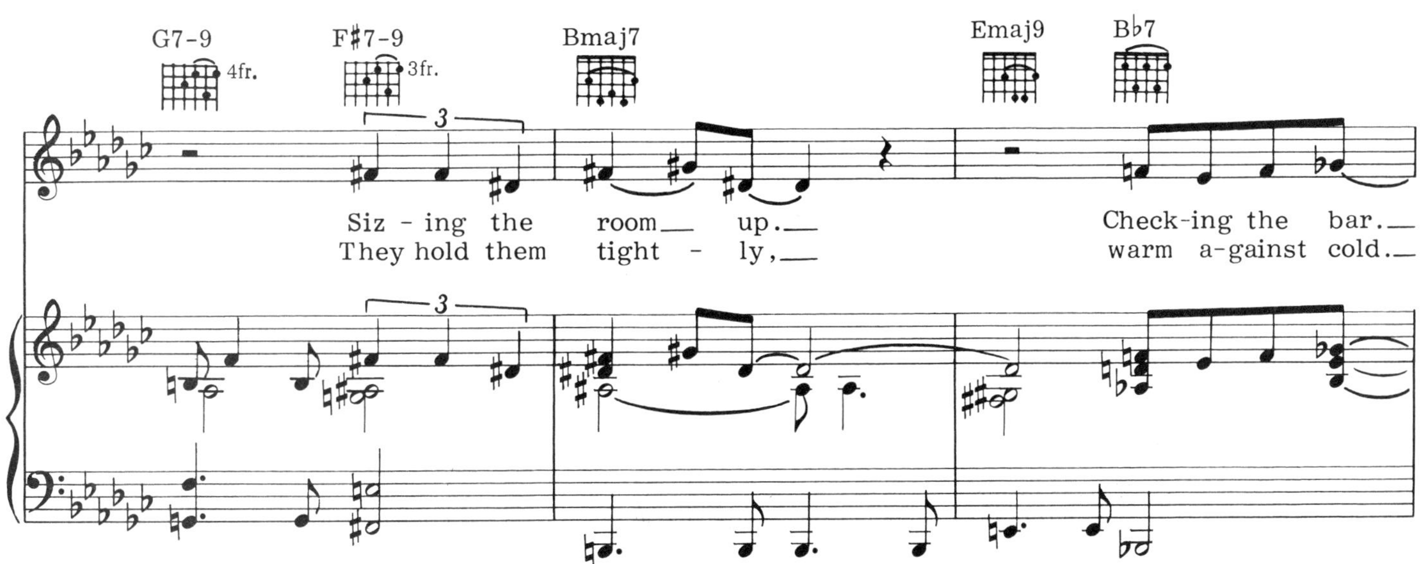

Ebm
Abm
Bbm
Ebm
Lo - cal girls' un - spo - ken con - ver - sa - tion. Mis - in - for - ma - tion. Plays gui - tar.
One more year of trav - 'ling 'round this cir - cuit. Then you can work it in - to gold.
Bb7/D
Dbmaj7
G7-9
F#7-9
Bm7
E7
Amaj7
C#7+5
They say Jo - nah, he was swal - lowed by a whale.
F#m7
Dmaj7
G#m7-5

C♯7-9
Fmaj7
Fm7-5
B♭7
E♭maj7
But I say there's no truth to that tale.
E♭7
A♭m7
4fr.
D♭7
4fr.
I know Jo - nah, he was swal-lowed by a song.
G♭maj7
1.
C♭maj7/B♭
4fr.
E♭m
6fr.
Fm/E♭
4fr.
E♭m
6fr.
Fm/E♭
4fr.
2.
C♭maj7/B♭
4fr.

E♭maj7
Here's to all the boys who came a -
A♭maj7
4fr.
Dm7-5
long, car - ry - ing soft
D♭maj7
4fr.
C7
3fr.
Fm7
gui - tars in card - board cas - es all
B♭7
Am7-5
4fr.
A♭maj7
4fr.
night long.

Fm7
Bb7
Am7-5
4fr.
Do you wonder where those boys have gone?
Abmaj7
4fr.
Fm7
Bb7
Do you wonder where those boys have gone?
Ebmaj7
Abmaj7
4fr.
Repeat and fade
Ebmaj7
Abmaj7
4fr.

Keep The Customer Satisfied

Words and Music by PAUL SIMON

Ab
4fr
Eb
It's the same old sto - ry (Yeah)
It's the same old sto - ry
Ev - 'ry-where I
Ab
4fr
Eb
Bb
Eb
go, I get slan - dered, Li - beled, I hear words
Ab
4fr
Eb
I nev - er heard in the Bi - ble. And I'm one step a-head of the
Cm
Eb
Cm
Ab
4fr
Eb
Eb7
shoe shine, Two steps a-way from the coun-ty line, Just trying to keep my cus-tom-ers

Ab
4fr
1.Eb
2.Eb
sat - is - fied, Sat - is - fied.
fied.
Ab
4fr
Woh
Woh
Woh
Woh
f
Eb/Ab
Eb
Ab
4fr
But it's the same old
Eb
Ab
4fr
sto - ry
Ev - 'ry-where I go, I get

Eb
Bb
Eb
slan - dered, Li - beled, I hear words I nev - er heard in the Bi -
Ab
4fr
Eb
Cm
ble. And I'm so tired, I'm
Eb
Cm
Bb
Eb
Eb7
oh so tired, But I'm trying to keep my cus - tom - ers
Ab
4fr
Eb
Ab7
sat - is - fied, Sat - is - fied.

The Late, Great Johnny Ace

Words and Music by PAUL SIMON

Coda by Philip Glass

G
G7
C
F/C
had - n't been play - ing that long. When a man came on the ra -
wait - ed till it came. It came all the way from Tex -
heard John Len - non died. And the two of us went to
C
C7
F
Gm7
F/A
B♭9
Am7
3 fr.
di - o, and this is what he said: he said, "I
as with a sad and sim - ple face. And they
this bar, and we stayed to close the place. And
Dm
E
Am7
F
hate to break it to his fans, but John - ny Ace is dead." (Yeah, yeah,
signed it on the bot - tom, "From the Late Great John - ny Ace." (Yeah, yeah,
ev - 'ry song we played was for the Late Great John - ny Ace. (Yeah, yeah,
Am
Dm7
To Coda
1. G
2. G
yeah.)
yeah.)
yeah.)
Well, I
rit.
a tempo

Medium shuffle
C
mf R.H.
C
It was the year of the Bea - tles. It was the
year of the Stones.
It was nine - teen six - ty - four.
I was liv -

B♭/D
Fm
E♭
C
B
B♭
Am
ing in Lon - don with the girl ___ from the sum - mer be - fore. ___
F♯°7
Fm7
G7-9
6
8
12
8
It was the
C
year of the Bea - tles. It was the year of the Stones. ___ A
year af - ter J. F. ___ K. ___

B♭/D
Fm
E♭
We were stay - ing up all night and
C
B
B♭
G
F
B♭9
giv - ing the days a - way.
And the
rit.
Freely
E♭maj7
A♭maj7
4fr.
E♭
B♭7-9
A♭maj7
Tempo I
mu - sic was flow - ing a - maz - ing and blow - ing my way.
mp
D7
3fr.
A♭maj7
4fr.
D7
3fr.
D. S. al Coda
On a

Coda
G
Medium tempo
Am/E
Bb/F
Am/E
Bb
Bbm/Db
Am/E
Bb/F
Bbm/Db
Am/E
1.
2.

Late In The Evening

Words and Music by PAUL SIMON

I could-n't of been no more than one or two.
I'm feel - in' all right. I'm with my boys. I'm with my troops,
fun - ky bar. And I stepped out - side to smoke my - self a "J."
3
F
yeah.
I re-
And
And
B♭
mem - ber there's a ra - di - o com - in' from the room
down a - long the av - e - nue, some guys were shoot - in' pool,
when I came back to the room, ev - 'ry - bod - y just
next door, and my moth - er laughed the way some la - dies do
and I heard the sound of a cap - pel - la groups,
seemed to move, and I turned my amp up loud and I be-gan to play.

F
yeah,
when it's
sing-in'
And it was
C
late in the eve - ning
and the mu - sic's seep-ing
late in the eve - ning,
and all the girls out on the
late in the eve - ning,
and I blew that room a -
F
1.2.
through.
The
stoops, yeah.
Then I
way.
3.
B♭

F
B♭
F
C

F
To Coda
B♭
The first thing I re-mem-ber when you came
in-to my life, I said, "I'm gon-na get that girl no mat-ter what I do."
F
Well, I

B♭
guess I'd been in love __ be-fore, __ and once or twice __ I been on __ the floor, __ but I
F
nev-er loved no one __ the way __ that I __ loved you. __
C
And it was late in the eve - ning, __
F
and all __ the mu - sic seep - ing through. __

F
D.S. 𝄋 al Coda
Coda
Repeat and fade
F

Loves Me Like A Rock

Words and Music by PAUL SIMON

C
G
G7
C
boy. (When I was just a boy.) I'm a sing - er in the Sun - day choir,
G
D
Oh, my ma - ma loves me, she loves me. She
G
Em
C
get down on her knees and hug me like She Loves Me Like A
3
3
G
C
F
C
Rock. She rocks me like the rock of a - ges and loves

G
me.
She love me, love me, love me, love me.
No chord
G
C
2. When I was grown to be a man, (Grown to be a
G
C
man.) and the dev - il would call my name. (Grown to be a
G
C7
man.) I'd say, "Now who do, who do you think you're fool -

G
C
G
- ing?" (Grown to be a man.) I'm a con - sum - mat - ed
C
G
G7
C
man, (Grown to be a man.) I can snatch a lit - tle pu - ri - ty, -
G
D
My ma - ma loves me, she loves me. She
G
Em
C
get down on her knees and hug me like She Loves Me Like A

G
F
C
Rock. She rocks me like the rock of a - ges and loves
G
me. She love me, love me, love me, love me.
G
C
3. And if I was the Pres - i - dent, (Was the Pres - i -
G
C
dent.) the min - ute the Con - gress call my name. (Was the Pres - i -

G
C7
dent.) I say, "Now who do, who do you think you're fool -
G
C
G
(Who do you think you're fool - ing?")
- ing?" I've got the Pres - i - den - tial
C
G
Seal, (Was the Pres - i - dent.) I'm up on the Pres - i - den - tial
C
G
Po - di - um. My ma - ma loves me, she loves

D
G
Em
me. She get down on her knees and hug me like She
C
G
C
Loves Me Like A Rock. She rocks me like the
F
C
G
rock of a-ges and loves me. She love me, love me, love me,
Fade out
(Love me like a rock.)
love me. She love me, love me, love me, love me.
(Love me like a

Mother And Child Reunion

Words and Music by PAUL SIMON

Em
oh, lit - tle dar - ling of mine.
1. I can't for the
2. I just can't be -
D
life of me
lieve it's so,
re - mem - ber a sad - der day,
and though it seems strange to say,
Em
D
I know they say let it be,
I nev - er been laid so low
But it just don't work
in such a mys -
Em
out that way,
te - ri - ous way,
C
And the course of a life - time runs
And the course of a life - time runs

D

o - ver and o - ver a - gain. No, I
o - ver and o - ver a - gain. But I

C D G C D

would not give you false hope on this strange and mourn - ful

G C D G Em

day, When the Moth - er And Child Re - u - nion is

Am G D

on - ly a mo - tion a - way, Oh, oh the

C D G C D
Moth-er And Child Re-u-nion is on-ly a mo-tion a-way,
G C D
Oh, the Moth-er And Child Re-
G Em Am G D
u-nion is on-ly a mo-ment a-way.
G

My Little Town

Words and Music by PAUL SIMON

A
Bm
E
A
wall. Lord, I re - call my lit - tle town:
A/G♯
F♯m
Am6
4fr
D9
Com - ing home af - ter school; rid - ing my bike past the gates of the fac -
G
E7
F
B♭
to - ries; my mom do - ing the
F
F+
A
D
laun - dry, hang - ing our shirts in the dirt - y breeze.
cresc.

G
And af - ter it rains there's a rain -
mf
D
bow, and all of the col - ors are black. It's
3
Em
D
G
not that the col - ors aren't there; it's just i - mag - i - na -
Dmaj7
E
Em7
tion they lack. Ev - 'ry - thing's the same back

A
D
G
D
in my lit - tle town.
cresc.
G
D
C♯m7
4fr
Bm
Noth-ing but the dead and dy - ing back in my lit - tle town,
f
D
C♯m7
4fr
noth-ing but the dead and dy -
Bm
Tacet
ing back in my lit - tle town.

A
F♯m
Am6
4fr
In my lit - tle town
I nev - er meant noth -
mp
D9
4fr
G
E7
ing; I was just my fa - ther's son,
mm.
F
B♭
F
Sav - ing my mon - ey,
B♭
F
B♭
dream - ing of glo - ry;
twitch - ing like a

F
F+
A
D
fin - ger on the trig - ger of a gun!
cresc.
f
Repeat and fade
D
C♯m7
4fr
Bm
Leav-ing noth - ing but the dead and dy - ing back in my lit - tle town,
Repeat and fade
D
C♯m7
4fr
noth-ing but the dead and dy -
Bm
ing back in my lit - tle town.
Noth -

Oh, Marion

Words and Music by PAUL SIMON

G♯m
G♯m/F♯
G♯m/E♯
A♯o7
B
A
He said, "The more I get to
E
C♯m/E
Bm/E
C♯m/E
B
A
E
C♯m/E
Bm/E
think-ing, the less I tend to laugh."
C♯m/E
B
A
D6
D♯
The boy's got brains. He just ab - stains.
G♯m
G♯m/F♯
G♯m/E♯
C♯m/E
G♯m
G♯m/F♯
C♯m/E
D♯7
The

G♯m G♯m/F♯ G♯m/E♯ C♯m/E G♯m G♯m/F♯
4fr.
boy's got a heart, but it beats on his op-po-site side.
boy's got a voice, but the voice is his nat-u-ral dis-guise.
G♯m/E♯ C♯m/E G♯m G♯m/F♯ G♯m/E♯ C♯m/E
It's a strange phe-nom-e-non, the laws of na-ture de-fied.
Yes, the boy's got a voice, but his words don't con-nect to his eyes.
G♯m G♯m/F♯ G♯m/E♯ A♯º7 B A E C♯m/E Bm/E
He said, "It's a chance I had to take,
He says, "Ah, but when I sing,
C♯m/E B A E C♯m/E Bm/E
so I shift-ed my heart for its safe-ty's sake."
I can hear the truth au-di-tion-ing."

C♯m/E
B
A
D6
E♭
The boy's got a heart, but it beats on his op-po-site...
The boy's got a voice, but the voice is his nat-u-ral...
A♭
A♭/G
A♭/G♭
Fm7
4fr.
Oh, Mar-i-on, I think I'm in trou - ble here.
A°7
B♭m7
B♭m7-5
I should-'ve be-lieved you when I heard you say-
E♭7
A♭
Cm7
4fr.
3fr.
ing it: the on - ly time that love is an eas-

D♭m7
4fr.
B♭m7-5
B
y game
is when two
oth - er
F♯7
F𝄪°7
G♯m
G♯m/F♯
G♯m/E♯
C♯m/E
peo - ple
are play
- ing it.
1.
2.
D♯7
The
Repeat and fade

Old Friends

Words and Music by PAUL SIMON

Fm7
Bb7
Abmaj7
Gm7
Fm7
Bb7
Win - ter com - pan - ions, The old men Lost in their o - ver - coats,
Eb
Fm7
Cm
Fm7
Bb7
Wait - ing for the sun - set. The sounds of the cit - y,
Gm7
Cm
Bb
Sift - ing through trees, set - tle like dust On the
Ab
Eb6
Fm7
Bb7
shoul - ders Of the Old Friends. Can you im - a - gine us

E♭maj7 A♭ A♭m E♭
Years from to-day, Shar - ing a park bench qui - et - ly? How
Fm7 B♭7 Cm A♭maj7 E♭maj7
ter - ri - bly strange To be sev - en - ty. Old Friends,
Fm7 B♭7 A♭maj7 Gm7 Fm7 B♭7
mem - o - ry brush - es the same years. Si - lent - ly shar - ing the
E♭6 Cm A♭maj7 E♭maj7 A♭maj7 E♭maj7
same fears.
poco ritard

Punky's Dilemma

Words and Music by PAUL SIMON

Am
sion - al - ly plays L. A.
than an - y or - din-ar - y jam. I'm a
Fmaj7
Gm7
Fmaj7
1.
Cas - u - al - ly glanc - ing at his toup - ee.
cit - i - zens for boy-sen-ber-ry jam fan.
2.
Bb maj7
Ah, South Cal - i -
Fmaj7
Gm7
forn - ia.
If I be-come a First Lieu-ten - ant

C7
Fmaj7
Gm
would you put my pho — to on your pia-no?
To Mar-y Jane
Fmaj7
Bb
Best wish - es Mar - tin.
Old Rod - ger, draft dod - ger
Am
Fmaj7
Bb
leav - in' by the base-ment door.
Ev - 'ry-bod - y knows what he's
Bbmaj7
Bb6
Fmaj7
Gm7
tip - py toe - ing down there for.
Repeat and fade.

One Man's Ceiling Is Another Man's Floor

Words and Music by PAUL SIMON

G
hard feel - ings here a - bout some words that were said, Been some
mf light shuffle
G7
C7
hard feel - ings here, and what is more, There's been a blood - y pur - ple nose, And some
blood - y pur - ple clothes that were mess - in' up the lob - by
G
floor, It's just a - part - ment house rules, So all you

F
C
F
F♯dim
'part - ment house fools, re - mem - ber: One Man's Ceil - ing Is An -
G7
C
C7
F
F♯dim
G
oth - er Man's Floor! One Man's Ceil - ing Is An - oth - er Man's
Am
C7
Floor. There's been some strange go - in's on, And some
folks have come and gone, like the el - e - va - tor man don't work no

F7
more, I heard a rack - et in the hall, and I
thought I heard a call, But I nev - er o - pened up my door.
C
It's just a - part - ment house sense, It's like a -
B♭
F
B♭
Bdim
C7
F
part - ment house rents, re-mem - ber: One Man's Ceil - ing Is An-oth - er Man's Floor!

F7
B♭
Bdim
C
Dm
One Man's Ceil - ing Is An - oth - er Man's Floor!
Dm
A7
Dm
Gm7
There's an al - ley in the back of my build - ing where some
f heavy shuffle
Dm
A7
Dm
A
peo - ple con - gre - gate in shame. I was
Dm
A7
Dm
G
walk - ing with my dogs, and the night was black with smog, When I

F
A7
Dm
thought I heard some-bod-y call my name.
F
8va
mf Instrumental Solo
F7
B♭
(8va
loco
8va
loco
8va

F
E♭
B♭
E♭
Edim
Ah.
Re-mem-ber: One Man's Ceil-ing Is An-
loco
f
mf
F7
B♭
E♭
Edim
F
oth-er Man's Floor!
One Man's Ceil-ing Is An-oth-er Man's
Gm
Repeat and fade
Gm
F
C
B♭
Floor!
mp
Instrumental Solo
E♭
Gm
D7(omit 3rd)
Gm
No chord
f marcato

Rene and Georgette Magritte With Their Dog After The War

Words and Music by PAUL SIMON

F♯m6
E6/G♯
F♯m/A
Eas - i - ly los - ing their eve - ning clothes, they danced by the light of the
all of the man - ne - quins dressed in the style that brought tears to their im - mi - grant
B/A
E/G♯
moon to the Pen - guins, the
eyes, just like the Pen - guins, the
C♯m7
4 fr.
Amaj9
B9
Moon - glows, the O - ri - oles, the Five Sat - ins, the
Moon - glows, the O - ri - oles, the Five Sat - ins, the
E
G♯m7/D♯
C♯m7
E/B
Amaj7
deep for - bid - den mu - sic they'd been long - ing for, Re -
eas - y stream of laugh - ter flow - ing through the air, Re -

F♯m6
B9
E
1.
ne and Geor-gette Ma - gritte with their dog af - ter the war. Re -
ne and Geor-gette Ma - gritte with their dog a - près la guerre.
2.
F♯7
B
Amaj7
Side by side they fell a - sleep.
cresc.
mp
G♯m7
4 fr.
A6
E/G♯
B♯°7
Dec - ades glid - ing by like In - di-ans. Time is cheap.
C♯m7
4 fr.
A6
E/G♯
B7/F♯
When they wake up they will find

E
F♯7
B
F♯6/A♯
4fr.
all their per - son - al be - long - ings have
Amaj7
G♯m7
4fr.
F♯m6
in - ter - twined.
Oh,
N.C.
Re - ne and Geor - gette Ma - gritte with their dog af - ter the
p
E
N.C.
war were din - ing with the pow - er e -

Amaj7
lite and they looked in their bed-room drawer. And
F♯m6
E6/G♯
F♯m/A
what do you think they have hid - den a-way in the cab - i - net cold of their
F♯7/A♯
4fr.
G♯m
4fr.
hearts? The Pen - guins, the
freely
D♯m
6fr.
E
B
Moon - glows, the O - ri - oles, and the Five Sat - ins, for

E
G♯m7/D♯
4fr.
C♯m7
4fr.
E/B
Amaj7
now and ev - er af - ter as it was be - fore,
a tempo
D9-5
4fr.
F♯m/C♯
N.C.
Re - ne and Geor-gette Ma - gritte with their dog af - ter the
rit.
A6
E/G♯
F♯m6
E
war.
a tempo
A6
E/G♯
D♯°7/C
E

Richard Cory

Words and Music by PAUL SIMON

A
G
spread his wealth a - round
Born in - to so - ci -
Cor - y at a show.
And the ru - mor of his part
thanked him ver - y much,
So my mind was filled with won-
- e - ty, a bank - er's on - ly child, He had
- ies and the or - gies on his yacht! Oh, he
- der when the eve - ning head - lines read: "Rich - ard
Dm
C
F
A
ev - 'ry - thing a man could want: pow - er, grace and
sure - ly must be hap - py with ev - 'ry - thing he's
Cor - y went home last night and put a bul - let through his
F
F
Dm
style.
got. But I work in his fac - to - ry
head."

G
And I curse the life I'm liv-in' And I curse my pov-er-ty And I wish
F
Dm
that I could be, Oh, I wish that I could be, Oh, I wish
G
1.2.
Dm
that I could be Rich-ard Cor-y.
3.
Dm
2. The
3. He Cor-y.

St. Judy's Comet

Words and Music by PAUL SIMON

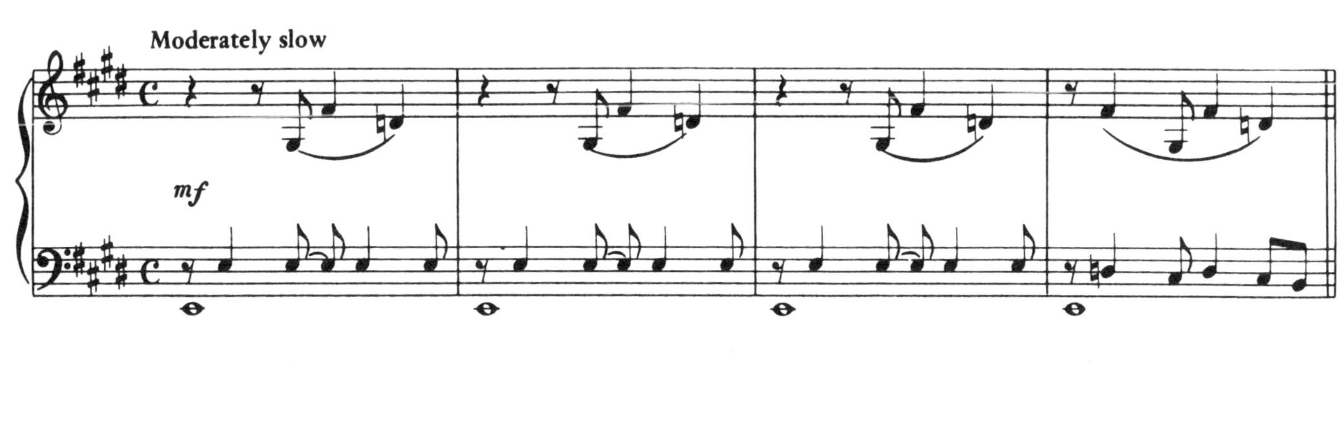

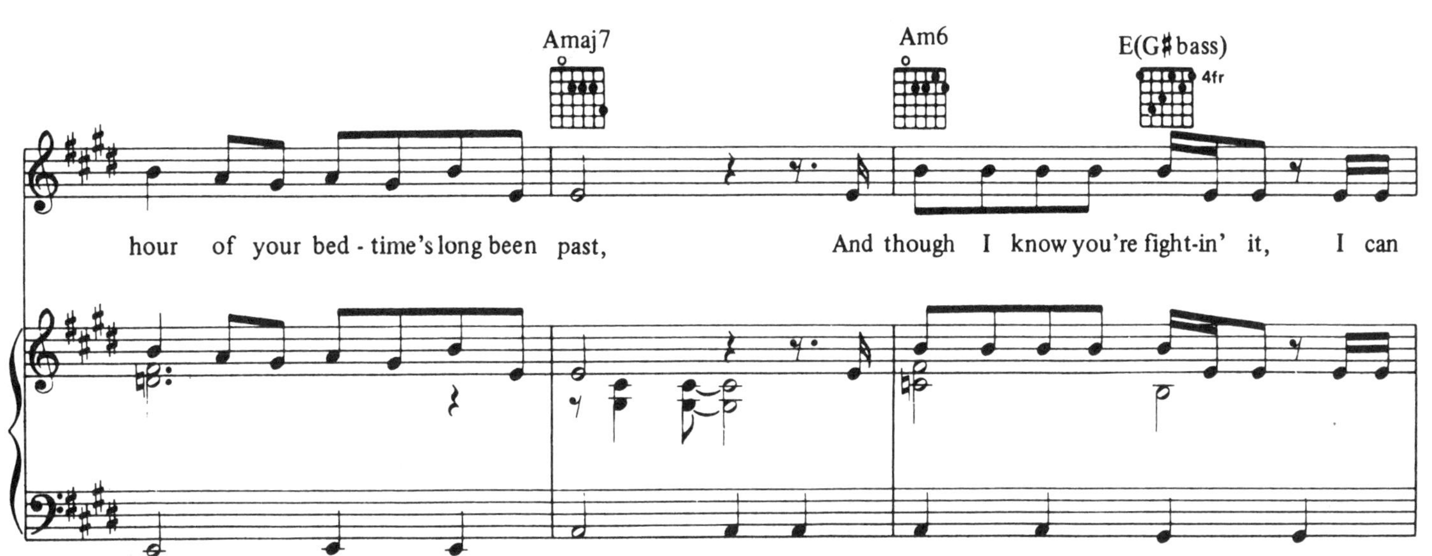

F♯m
B
E
F♯m
A
E9
tell when you rub your eyes, you're fad - in' fast, oh,_ fad - in' fast. Won't you
E9
run come see St. Ju - dy's Com - et roll a - cross the skies, And leave a spray of dia - monds in its
Amaj7
Am6
E(G♯ bass)
4fr
F♯m
B
E
F♯m
wake. I long to see St. Ju - dy's Com - et spar - kle in your eyes when you a -
A
E9
Amaj7
wake, oh, when you wake, wake.
Lit - tle boy,__
(Lit - tle boy, lit - tle

Am6
E(G♯bass)
4fr
E9
Won't you lay your bod - y down.
boy.)
Amaj7
Am6
E(G♯bass)
4fr
E9
Lit - tle boy,
Lit - tle boy, lit - tle boy,)
Won't you close your wear - y eyes.
G♯+5
G♯7
C♯m
Cm
Bm
B♭m
Ain't noth - in' flash - in' but the fire - flies.
A
E9
to Coda
Well, I

E9
sang it once,_ and I sang it twice, I'm goin' to sing it three times more, I'm goin' to
Amaj7
stay 'til your re - sis - tance is o - ver - come, 'Cause if
Am6
E(G♯ bass)
4fr
F♯m
B
E
F♯m
I can't sing my boy to sleep,_ well, it makes your fa - mous dad - dy look so
A
E9
D.S. al Coda
dumb, look so dumb. Won't you

Coda 𝄌

E9 E9

Oo, lit - tle sleep - y boy, do you know what time it is? Well, the hour of your bed - time's long been past,

Amaj7

And though I know you're fight - in' it, I can tell when you rub your eyes that you're fad - in' fast, oo, fad - in' fast.

Am6 E(G♯bass) 4fr F♯m B E F♯m

A E9

Fade out

Scarborough Fair/Canticle

Arrangement and original counter melody by PAUL SIMON and ARTHUR GARFUNKEL

Em
thyme.
Re - mem - ber
G
F♯m
Em
D
me to one who lives there.
Em
D
Em
D
Em
D
Ahead to next strain
Em
She once was a true love of mine.
Em
Fine
D
Em
mine.
rit.
p

Em
D
Em
D
Em
On the side of a hill in the deep for - est
On the side of a hill a sprink-ling of
War bel - lows blaz - ing in scar - let bat -
Tell her to make me a cam - bric shirt:
Tell her to find me an a - cre of land:
Tell her to reap it with a sick - le of leath - er:
G
Em
G
A
Em
green.
leaves.
tal - ions.
Trac - ing of spar - row on
Wash - es the grave with
Gen - er - als or - der their
Pars - ley, sage, rose - mar - y and thyme;
Pars - ley, sage, rose - mar - y and thyme;
Pars - ley, sage, rose - mar - y and thyme;
G
F♯m
Em
snow - crest - ed brown.
sil - ver - y tears.
sol - diers to kill.
Blan - kets and
A sol - dier
And to fight for a
With - out no seams nor nee - dle
Be - tween the salt wa - ter and the sea
And gath - er it all in a bunch of

D
Em
D
Em
D
Em
D
bed - clothes the child of the moun - tain.
cleans and po - lish - es a gun.
cause they've long a - go for - got - ten.
work,
strands,
heath - er,
Then she'll be a true love of
Then she'll be a true love of
Then she'll be a true love of
1.2.
Em
Sleeps un - a - ware of the clar - i - on call.
mine.
mine.
3.
Em
D.S. al Fine
mine.

Some Folk's Lives Roll Easy

Words and Music by PAUL SIMON

F♯m
B
E
G♯7sus4
4fr
stum - ble
Lord, ___
they
fall ___
through no
mp
G♯7
4fr
C♯m7
4fr
Cm7
3fr
Bm7
fault
of
their ___
own; ___
most folks
nev - er
E
A
3
catch
their ___
stars.
Bm
E
And here
I
am
Lord, _
I'm
knock - ing
at your
place _
of
mf

A
D9
4fr
G♯
4fr
C♯
4fr
bus' - ness;
I know I ain't got no bus' - ness here.
3
F♯7-9
3fr
Bm
Em7
A9
But you said if I ev - er got
5
Dmaj7
Gmaj7
C♯
4fr
F♯
so low I was bust - ed, you could be
B
E
trust - ed.
Some folks' lives roll
cresc.
f

A
D9
4fr
E
G♯7sus4
4fr
G♯7
4fr
eas - y; some folks' lives nev - er roll at
C♯m
4fr
E/B
A
G♯7
4fr
all, oh, they just
C♯m
4fr
F♯m
fall, they just fall,
dim.
B7
E
A
D9
4fr
E
some folks' lives.
rit.

Still Crazy After All These Years

Words and Music by PAUL SIMON

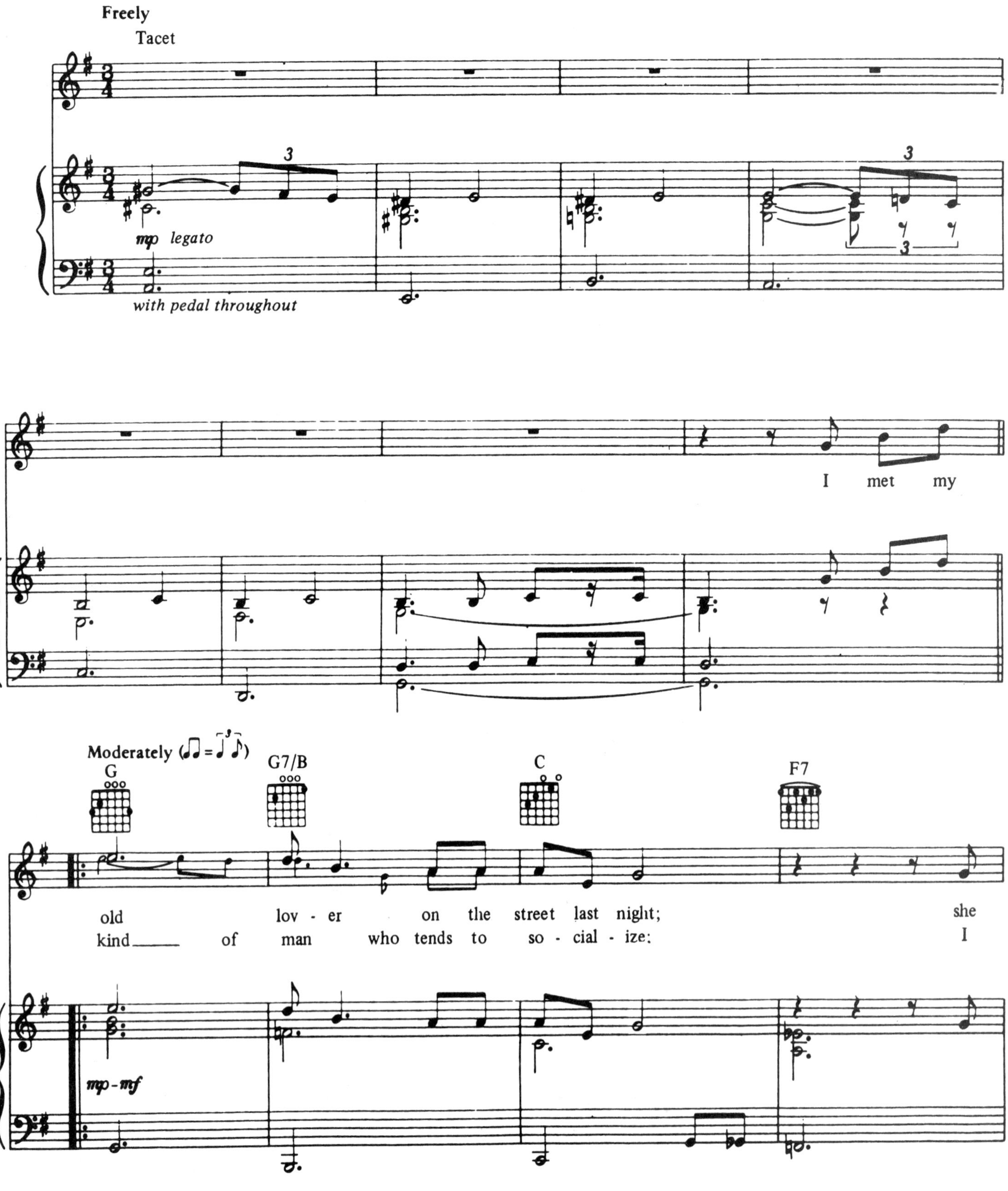

I met my

Moderately (♩♩ = ♩♪ triplet)

G G7/B C F7

old lov - er on the street last night; she
kind of man who tends to so - cial - ize: I

mp-mf

G F#°7 Bsus4 B7 Em7 E♭m7
seemed so glad to see me, I just smiled. And we
seem to lean on old fa - mil - iar ways. And I
Dm7 G7 C C#°7
talked a - bout some old times and we drank__ our - selves some beers.__
ain't no fool for love songs that whis - per in my__ ears.__
Still
G D7 Em C#°7
cra - zy__ af - ter all these__ years; oh, still
G/D D7 1.Cm 3fr
cra - zy__ af - ter all these__ years.
mf

D7
G
C
G
2. G9
3fr
I'm not the years.
gradual cresc.
Amaj7
Four in the morn - ing;
f
E
Em
G♯m7
4fr
C♯sus4
C♯
crapped out, yawn - ing; long - ing my life a -
F♯maj7
Em7
B
C
way. I'll nev - er wor - ry;

B C G G7 C
why should I?
It's all gon - na
decresc.
B C B C
fade.
mp
B Am7 G G G7/B
Now I sit by my win - dow and I
C F7 G F♯°7
watch the cars;
I fear I'll do some dam - age one fine

Bsus4
B7
E
D/E
A
A7/C♯
day. But I would not be con - vict - ed by a
cresc.
mf
D
D♯°7
A
E
E♯°7
ju - ry of my peers. Still cra - zy af - ter all these
F♯m
D♯°7
A
years; oh, still cra - zy, still
f
D
A/E
E7
A
D
A
cra - zy, still cra - zy af - ter all these years.
rit.
mp

The Sound Of Silence

Words and Music by PAUL SIMON

Dm
F
C
mains
with - in The
Sound
Of
Dm
Dm
C
Si - lence.
(2.) In rest - less dreams I walked a - lone
(3.) And in the nak - ed light I saw
mp (Melody)
Dm
F
nar - row streets of cob - ble - stone,
ten thou - sand peo - ple, may - be more.
'Neath the ha - lo of a
Peo - ple talk - ing with - out
Bb
F
Bb
F
street lamp,
speak - ing,
I turned my col - lar to the cold and damp
peo - ple hear - ing with - out lis - ten - ing

Bb
F
When my eyes were stabbed by the flash of a ne - on light that split the
Peo - ple writ - ing songs that voi - ces nev - er share and no one
Dm
F
C
Dm
night and touched The Sound Of Si - lence.
dare dis - turb The Sound Of Si - lence.
Dm
C
Dm
(4.) "Fools!" said I, "You do not know si - lence like a can - cer grows."
mf
F
Bb
F
"Hear my words that I might teach you, Take my arms that I might

B♭
F
B♭
reach you." But my words like si - lent rain- drops
F
Dm
F
C
fell, and ech- oed in the wells of
Dm
C
si - lence. (5.) And the peo - ple bowed and prayed
Dm
F
to the ne - on god they made. And the sign flashed out its

Bb
F
Bb
F
warn - ing. In the words that it was form - ing,
Bb
And the signs said "The words of the proph - ets are writ - ten on the sub - way
F
Dm
F
walls and ten - e - ment halls" And whis - per'd in The
poco a poco dim.
mp
C
Dm
Sounds Of Si - lence.
poco a poco ritard.
(Melody)
p
pp

Take Me To The Mardi Gras

Words and Music by PAUL SIMON

C
No·chord
mu - sic in the street both night and day.
Hur - ry, Take Me To The
C
G7
Mar - di Gras,
In the cit - y of my dreams,
You can le - gal - ize your laws, you can wear your sum-mer clothes in the New Or -
C
C7
F
leans.
And I will lay my bur-den down,

F9
Rest my head up - on that shore,
And when I wear that star - ry
E♭
Gm
crown,
I won't be want - ing an - y - more.
G7
No chord
Take your bur - dens to the
C
G7
Mar - di Gras,
Let the mu - sic wash your soul,

You can mingle in the street, You can jingle in the beat of the jelly roll.
C
No chord
C
Tumba, tumba, tumba, Mardi Gras,
G7
Tumba, tumba, tumba day,
Mm
C
Mm

That Was Your Mother

Words and Music by PAUL SIMON

F
great, I held this job as a trav - el - ing
Day. I said, "Good gra - cious, can this be
great. You are the bur - den of my gen - er -
C
sales - man that kept me mov - ing from state to state
my luck? If that's my prayer book, Lord, let us pray."
a - tion. I sure do love you. Let's get that straight.
F
F
Well, I'm stand - ing on the cor - ner of La -
Well, I'm stand - ing on the cor - ner of La -
Well, I'm stand - ing on the cor - ner of La -

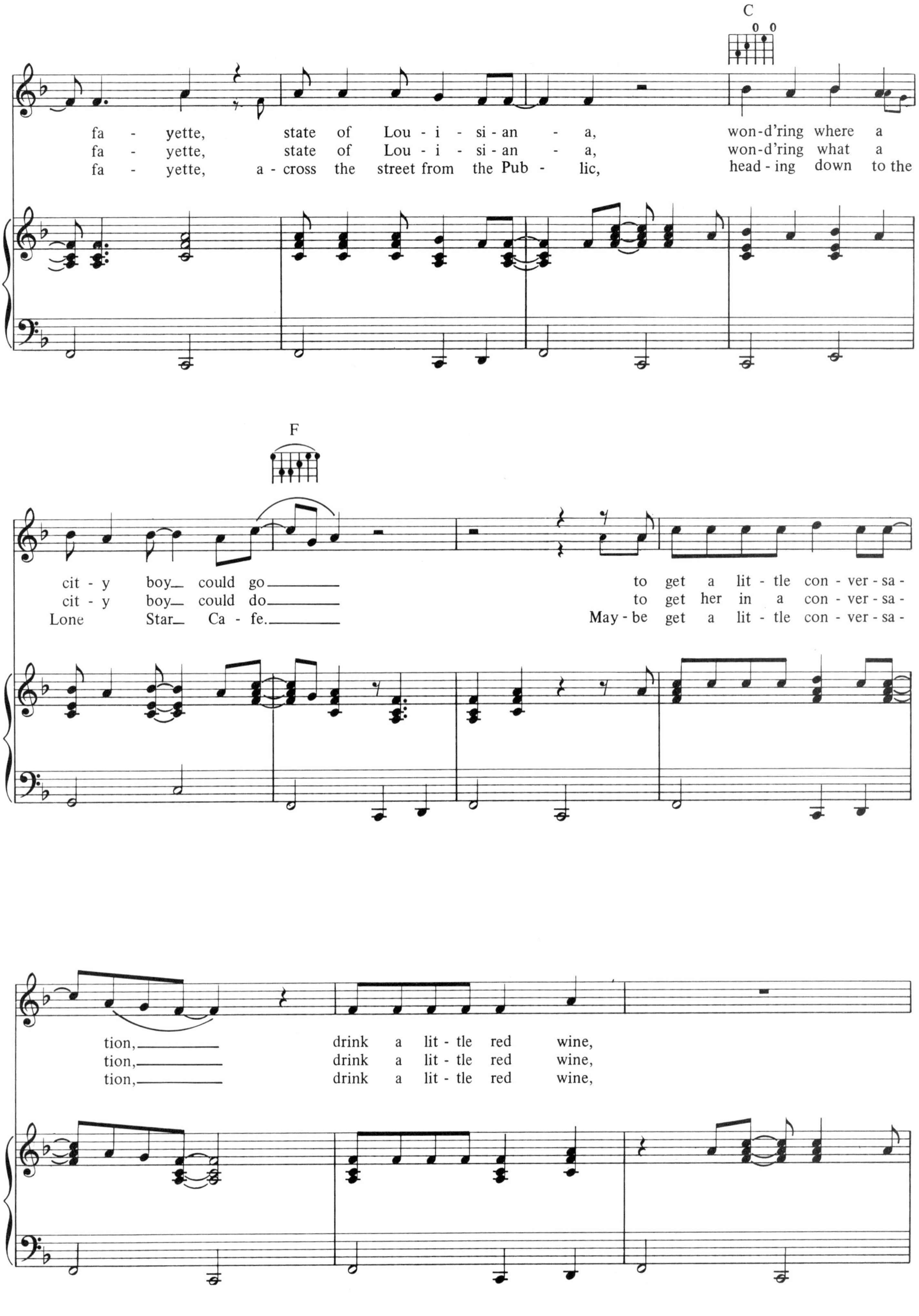

C

fa - yette, state of Lou - i - si - an - a, won-d'ring where a
fa - yette, state of Lou - i - si - an - a, won-d'ring what a
fa - yette, a - cross the street from the Pub - lic, head - ing down to the

F

cit - y boy could go to get a lit - tle con - ver - sa -
cit - y boy could do to get her in a con - ver - sa -
Lone Star Ca - fe. May - be get a lit - tle con - ver - sa -

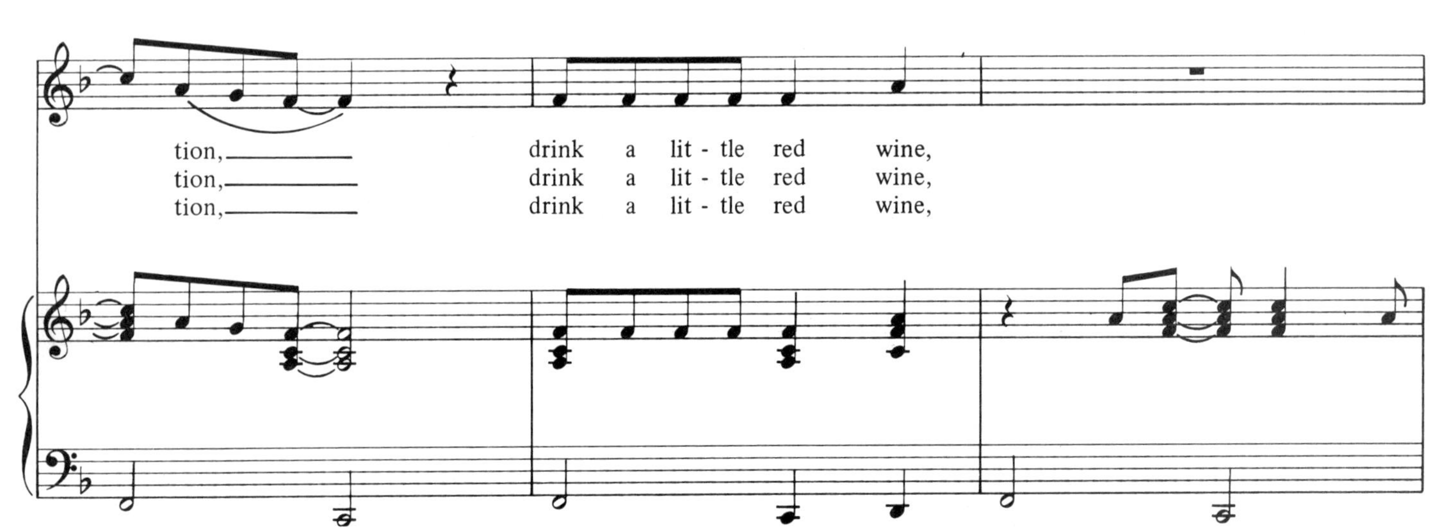

C
F
catch a lit - tle bit of those Ca - jun girls dancing to Zy - de - co.
dance to the mu - sic of Clif - ton Chen-ier, the King of the Ba - you.
stand - ing in the shad - ow of Clif - ton Chen-ier danc - ing the night a - way.
1.2.
A - long comes a
Well, that was your
3.
C
F
C/E
F

Train In The Distance

Words and Music by PAUL SIMON

B♭m/D♭
C7
Fm7
South - ern skies the night he met her. She was mar - ried to some -
boy and the girl get mar - ried. Sure e - nough they have a
wom - an re - main in con - tact, let us say it's for the
B♭9
E♭
B♭/D
one. He was dog - ged - ly de -
son. And though they both were oc - cu -
child, with dis - a - gree - ments a - bout the
B♭m/D♭
C7
Fm7
ter - mined that he would get her. He was old, he was young.
pied with the child she car - ried, dis - a - gree - ments had be -
mean - ing of a mar - riage con - tract, con - ver - sa - tions hard and

A♭/E♭
E♭
D♭/E♭
From time to time he'd tip his heart,
gun. And in a while they just fell a - part.
wild. But from time to time he makes her laugh,
A♭/E♭
A♭
4 fr.
E♭maj7/G
but each time she with - drew.
It was - n't hard to do.
she cooks a meal or two.
E♭
D♭/E♭
A♭/E♭
E♭m7
Ev - 'ry - bod - y loves the sound of a train in the dis-tance. Ev - 'ry - bod - y thinks it's
E♭
D♭/E♭
A♭/E♭
true. Ev - 'ry-bod - y loves the sound of a train in the dis - tance.

1.
Ebm7
Eb
Db/Eb
Ev - 'ry - bod - y thinks_ it's true.
Ab/Eb
Ebm7
2.
Eb
Ev - 'ry - bod - y thinks_ it's
true.
Db maj9
3 fr.
Cm7
3 fr.
Two dis - ap - point - ed be - liev - ers,_
What is the point of this sto - ry?_
B°7
Cm7/Bb
A9-5
4 fr.
Ab
4 fr.
two peo-ple play - ing the game._
What in - for - ma - tion per - tains?_
Ne - go - ti - a - tions and
The thought that life could be

Eb/G
Gb
Db/F
Cb
To Coda
love songs are of - ten mis - tak - en for one and the same.
bet - ter is wo - ven in - del - i - bly in - to our hearts
Bb11
D. S. (no repeats) al Coda
Coda
Bb11
Eb
Db/Eb
and our brains.
Ab/Eb
Ebm7
(Like a train in the dis - tance.)
Repeat and fade
Eb
Db/Eb
Ab/Eb
Ebm7

Under African Skies

Words and Music by PAUL SIMON

Eb/Bb Bb Eb Ab Eb/Bb Bb
moon shone in his eyes. His
'round my nurs - er - y door. I said,
Eb Ab Eb/Bb Bb Eb Ab
path was marked by the stars in the south-ern hem - i -
"Take this child, Lord, from Tuc - son, Ar - i - zon -
Eb/Bb Bb Eb Ab Eb/Bb Bb
sphere, and he walked his days un - der Af - ri - can
a. Give her the wings to fly through har - mo - ny and she won't
Eb Ab To Coda Eb/Bb Bb Eb Ab
skies.
both - er you no more."
This is the sto - ry of how
mf

Eb/Bb
Bb
Eb
Ab
4fr.
we be - gin to re - mem - ber.
This is the pow - er - ful puls - ing of love in the vein.
Af - ter the dream of fall - ing and call - ing your
name out,
these are the roots of rhy - thm,

Eb/Bb Bb Eb Ab 4fr. | 1. Eb/Bb Bb

and the roots of rhy-thm re - main.

Eb Ab Eb/Bb Bb Eb Ab

Eb/Bb Bb | 2. Eb/Bb Bb Eb Ab

In Ka - oom - ba oom - ba

Eb/Bb Bb Eb Ab Eb/Bb Bb

oom - ba oh. 'Ka -

Eb
Ab
4fr.
Eb/Bb
Bb
oom - ba oom - ba oom - ba oh.
Ka -
D.S. (lyric 1) al Coda
Coda
Repeat and fade

THE BOY IN THE BUBBLE

WORDS BY PAUL SIMON
MUSIC BY PAUL SIMON AND FORERE MOTLOHELOA

A5
C
D
A5
C
D
C
D
slow day and the sun__ was beat - ing on the sol- diers by the side of the road.__
dry wind and it swept_ a - cross the des - ert and curled in - to the cir - cle of birth.__
turn - a - round jump-shot, it's ev - 'ry - bod - y jump-start, it's ev - 'ry gen - er - a - tion throws a
C
D
A5
C
D
There was a bright light, a shat - ter - ing of shop win-dows, the
And the dead sand was fall - ing on the chil - dren, the
he - ro up the pop-charts. Med - i - cine is mag - i - cal and mag - i - cal is art. There go the
A5
C
D
C
D
C
D
G
bomb in the ba - by car-riage was wired_ to the ra - di - o.__ These are the days_ of mir -
moth-ers and the fa - thers and the au - to - mat - ic earth. These are the days_ of mir -
boy in the bub - ble and the ba - by with the ba - boon heart._ These are days_ of la -

C
D
G
x000
a - cle and won - der. This is the long— dis - tance call.
a - cle and won - der. This is the long— dis - tance call.
sers in the jun - gle, la - sers in the jun - gle some - where.
The way the cam - er - a fol - lows us in slo - mo, the way we look to us all,—
The way the cam - er - a fol - lows us in slo - mo, the way we look to us all,—
Stac - ca - to sig - nals of con - stant in - for - ma - tion, a loose af - fil - i - a - tion of mil -
the way we look to a dis - tant con - stel - la - tion that's
the way we look to a dis - tant con - stel - la - tion that's
lion-aires and bil - lion - aires and ba - by: These are the days of mir - a - cle and won - der.

G
C
D
C
D
C
D
G
dy - ing in a cor - ner of the sky.
dy - ing in a cor - ner of the sky.
This is the long dis - tance call.
These are the days of mir -
These are the days of mir -
The way the cam - er - a fol -
C
D
G
C
D
C
D
1.2.
C
D
a - cle and won - der and don't cry, ba - by, don't cry, don't cry.
a - cle and won - der and don't cry, ba - by, don't cry, don't cry.
lows us in slo - mo, the way we look to us all,
3
C
D
G
C
D
oh yeah.
The way we look to a dis - tant con - stel - la - tion that's dy -

G
C
D
x000
0 0
0
ing in a cor - ner of the sky.
These are the days— of mir -
3
a - cle and won - der and don't— cry, ba - by, don't cry,— don't cry,— don't cry.
Repeat and fade

You're Kind

Words and Music by PAUL SIMON

A6
A9
D
good, you're so good; you in-tro-duced me to your neigh-bor-hood.
A
D
A
E
Seems like I ain't nev-er had so man-y friends be-fore; that's be-cause you're good, you're so
A
Bmaj7
E
good. Why you don't treat me like the oth-er hu-mans do is just a
A7
E
Bmaj7
mys-ter-y to me. It gets me ag-i-tat-ed
3

E
A9
F♯
when I think that you're gon - na love me now in - def - i - nite - ly So good -
B
A9
E
bye, good - bye, I'm gon - na leave you now and here's the rea - son why: I like to
B9
E
B
F♯
sleep with the win - dow o - pen and you keep the win - dow closed. So good - bye, good - bye, good -
B
E7
B9
bye. Oh, oh, oh, oh,

B7
E7
B9
oh, oh, oh, oh,
doot doot doot doot doot oh, oh,
F♯6
doo doo doo doo doo
D. S. 𝄋 (instrumental) and fade
B
A6
A9
doo doo.